GET TO KNOW ANIMALS ... of the JUNGLE

The Center for Science Teaching and Learning

Red Penguin
BOOKS

Get To Know Animals of the Jungle
Copyright © 2021 by The Center for Science Teaching and Learning
Illustrations by Ellen Valentino
Published by Red Penguin Books
Bellerose Village, New York
Library of Congress Control Number: 2021912891
ISBN
Print 978-1-63777-093-1/978-1-63777-094-8
Digital 978-1-63777-095-5

Animals are amazing! They live all over the world and they all look very different from one another. Some are plant eaters, some are meat eaters, and some eat both! But do you know what a female, male, baby and a group of each type of animal is called? Many animals have different names for each and some are very interesting while some are really funny!

Jungles are thick tropical forests with many plants and vines powered by bright sunlight. This light helps the plants and trees grow. In fact, they grow so much that it can be very difficult to move around in a jungle. Jungles are humid places, because the forests are so thick that when they release water into the air, they make their own clouds.

Apes

Any of various tailless semi-erect primates of Africa and southeastern Asia (such as the chimpanzee, gorilla, orangutan, or gibbon).

Where they live: Africa (gorillas and chimpanzees) and Asia (orangutans and gibbons).

Types of environment: Jungles, mountainous areas, savannahs, evergreen tropical rainforests, and monsoon forests. Most apes like hot climates and rarely venture out of tropical areas.

Diet: Apes are herbivores for the most part, eating leaves and fruit. They may also sometimes eat small animals and insects to add extra protein to their diet, especially younger apes. Adult chimpanzees are known to form packs to hunt monkeys.

What Do You Call ...

a male ape?
Male

a female ape?
Female

a baby ape?
Infant or Baby

a group of apes?
Shrewdness

Crocodile

Large semi-aquatic reptiles, they are the largest and heaviest of present day reptiles, growing up to 20 feet in length and up to about 2,200 pounds.

Where they live: Throughout the tropics in Africa, Asia, the Americas and Australia.

Types of Environment: Near lakes, rivers, wetlands and even some saltwater regions.

Diet: Crocodiles are carnivores, which means they only eat meat. In the wild, they feast on fish, birds, frogs and crustaceans; larger species eat large mammals. At the zoo, they eat small animals that have already been killed for them, such as rats, fish or mice. They also eat live locusts.

What Do You Call ...

a male crocodile?
Bull or Male

a female crocodile?
Cow or Female

a baby crocodile?
Hatchling

a group of crocodiles?
Bask

Frog

Frogs are any member of a diverse and largely carnivorous group of short-bodied, tailless amphibians.

Where they live: On all continents of the world, except for Antarctica.

Types of environment: Freshwater habitats, such as ponds, lakes, streams, rivers, and creeks.

Diet: Small frogs eat insects such as flies and moths, as well as snails, slugs and worms. They use long tongues and sticky saliva to catch prey that passes them by. Tadpoles eat algae in the ponds they grow in. As they grow, they feed on plants and small insects.

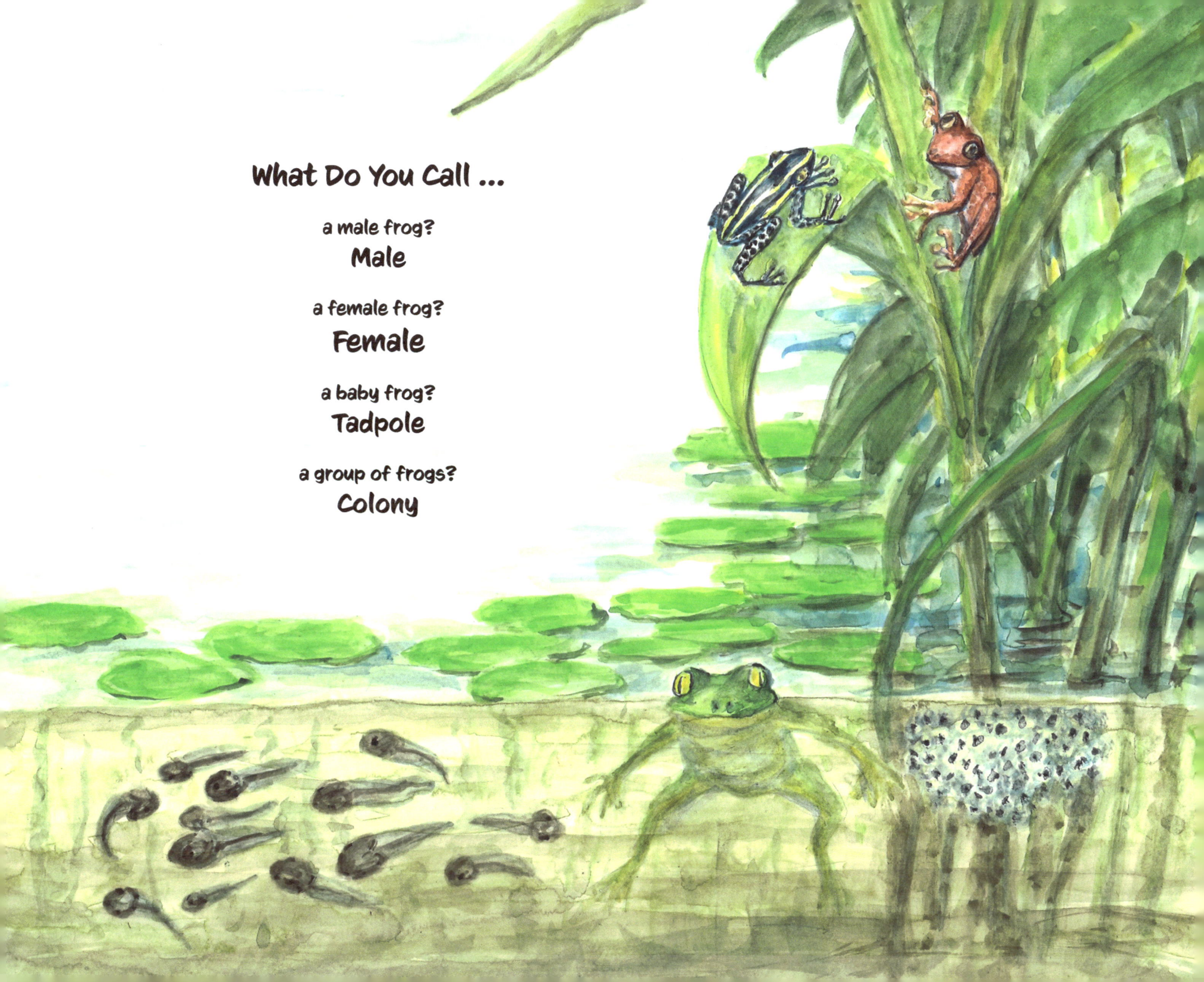

What Do You Call ...

a male frog?
Male

a female frog?
Female

a baby frog?
Tadpole

a group of frogs?
Colony

Gorillas

Ground-dwelling, predominantly herbivorous apes.

Where they live: In the forests of central sub-Saharan Africa.

Types of environment: Forests, where gorillas live in family groups of usually five to 10, but sometimes two to more than 50, led by a dominant adult male – or silverback –who holds his position for years.

Diet: Gorillas stick to a mainly vegetarian diet, feeding on stems, bamboo shoots and fruits. Western lowland gorillas, however, also have an appetite for termites and ants, and break open termite nests to eat the larvae.

What Do You Call ...

a male gorilla?
Male

a baby gorilla?
Infant or Baby

a female gorilla?
Female

a group of gorillas
Troop

Hippopotamus

Also known as the "river horse."

Where they live: Along the rivers and lakes throughout sub-Saharan Africa.

Types of environment: Underwater during the day (to escape the heat) and ashore at night (to feed).

Diet: Hippopotami feed on soft grasses and fallen fruit; they are also known to feed on meat from already dead animals, or occasionally even on small live mammals.

What Do You Call ...

a male hippopotamus?
Bull

a female hippopotamus?
Cow

a baby hippopotamus?
Calf

a group of hippopotami
Bloat or Herd

Monkeys

There are many species of monkey throughout much of the world.

Where they live: New World monkeys live in Central and South America, including the Amazon Rainforest. Old World monkeys live in the forests and plains of Asia and Africa. The Japanese snow monkey is one of the only primates that lives in a snowy climate.

Types of Environment: Most monkeys live in tropical forests. However, baboons live in drier places like the savannahs of Africa. Japanese snow monkeys live in northern Japan where it snows for many months out of the year. Snow monkeys keep warm by relaxing in hot springs, which are abundant in northern Japan.

Diet: Most monkeys eat a combination of grubs, insects, fruit, nuts, and plants. Larger monkeys may also eat larger prey, such as lizards. They may also steal bird eggs.

What Do You Call ...

a male monkey?
Male

a female monkey?
Female

a baby monkey?
Infant or Baby

a group of monkeys?
Troop

Mouse (plural: mice)

Mouse is a common name for many types of small rodent having a pointed snout, small rounded ears, a body-length scaly tail, and a high breeding rate. It is also a popular pet.

Where they live: Different habitats, such as forests, open grasslands, farms, on the borders of streams, swamps and ponds, rocky mountains and city settings.

Types of Environment: Habitats with moisture and humidity, such as those surrounding water sources, or, like the pocket mouse, in arid desert environments. Mice territories commonly overlap, especially if there are numerous species of mice in one area.

Diet: Mice eat mostly fruits, seeds and grains. They are omnivorous, which means they eat both plants and meat, and the common house mouse will eat just about anything it can find.

What Do You call ...

a male mouse?
Buck or Male

a female mouse?
Doe or Female

a baby mouse?
Pup or Pinkie

a group of mice?
Hoarde or Mischief

Parrots

Parrots are found mostly in tropical and subtropical regions.

Where they live: Southern Hemisphere, though they can be found in many other regions of the world, such as northern Mexico. Australia, South America and Central America have the greatest diversity of parrot species.

Types of environment: Mostly in warm areas, but occasionally in snowy climates (maroon-fronted parrots, thick-billed parrots and keas).

Diet: Parrots consume both meat and plants, mostly nuts, flowers, fruit, buds, and seeds. They have strong jaws that allow them to snap open nutshells.

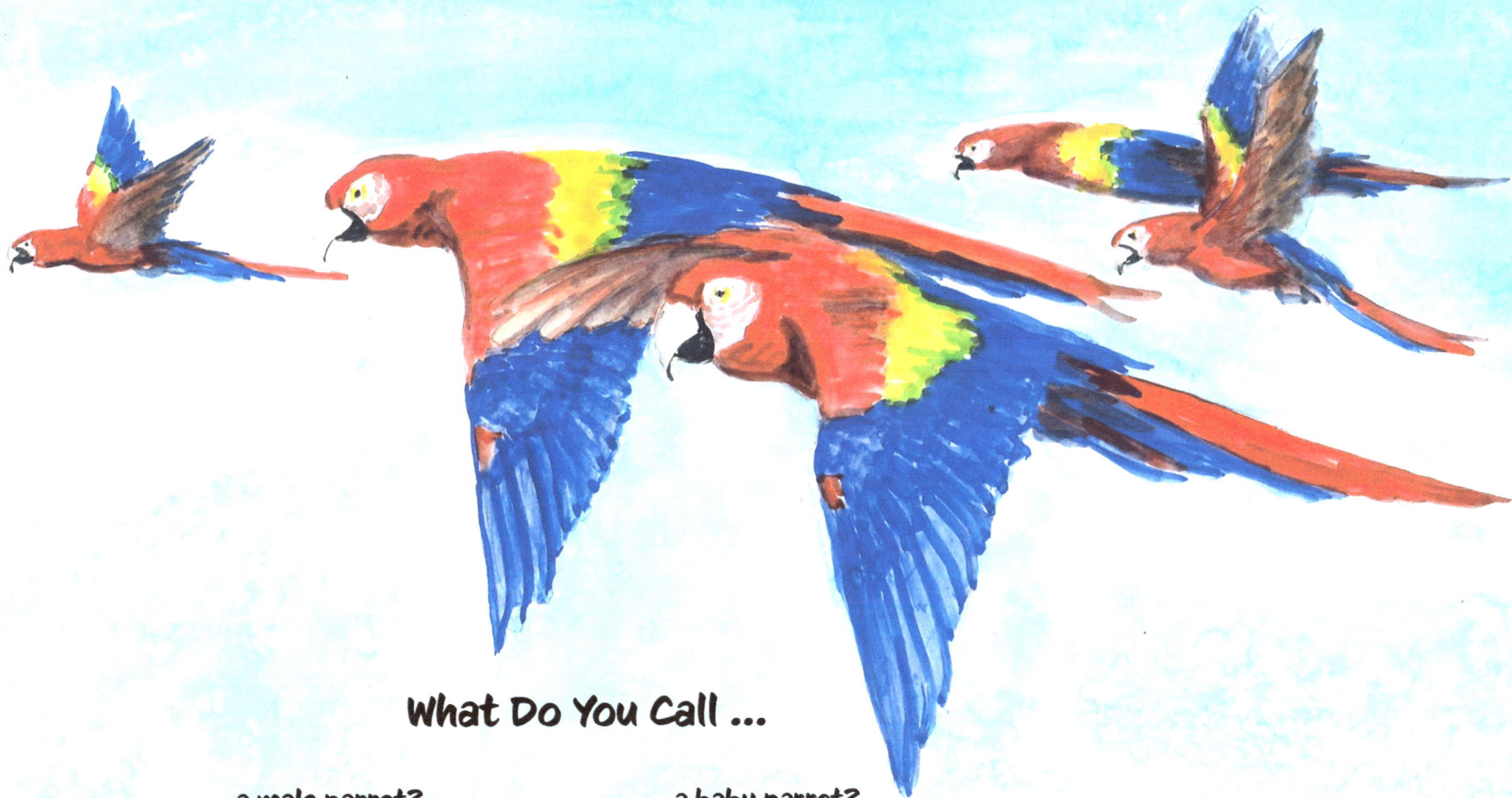

What Do You Call ...

a male parrot?
Cock or Male

a baby parrot?
Chick

a female parrot?
Hen or Female

a group of parrots?
Company or Flock

Tiger
The largest member of the cat family.

Where they live: Asia, including northern, colder areas, such as eastern Russia and northeastern China.

Types of environment: Rainforests, grasslands, savannas and even mangrove swamps.

Diet: Tigers eat a variety of prey ranging in size from termites to elephant calves. But they mostly eat large animals such as moose, deer, pigs, cows, horses, buffalos and goats.

What Do You Call ...

a male tiger?
Tiger

a female tiger?
Tigress

a baby tiger?
Cub

a group of tigers?
Ambush or Streak

Turtles

Reptiles with hard shells that protect them from predators.

Where they live: On every continent except Antarctica, including southeastern North America and South Asia.

Types of Environment: Just about everywhere in a number of habitats - ponds, streams, marshes or swamps.

Diet: Terrestrial turtles eat a variety of foods, from earthworms, grubs, snails, beetles and caterpillars to grasses, fruit, berries, mushrooms and flowers.

What Do You Call ...

a male turtle?
Male

a female turtle?
Female

a baby turtle?
Hatchling

a group of turtles?
Bale

Viper

Any of more than 200 species of venomous snakes (family Viperidae). All vipers are venomous and have long, hinged fangs.

Where they live: Mountains, rainforests, fields and deserts, with the exceptions of Antarctica, Australia, New Zealand, Madagascar, north of the Arctic Circle and island clusters such as Hawaii.

Types of Environment: Mostly tropical areas, particularly South America and Africa.

Diet: Vipers eat small animals and hunt by striking their prey. Vipers eat a variety of food, depending on the size of the snake. Prey includes small mammals, birds, lizards and eggs. When their prey is dead, they swallow it whole.

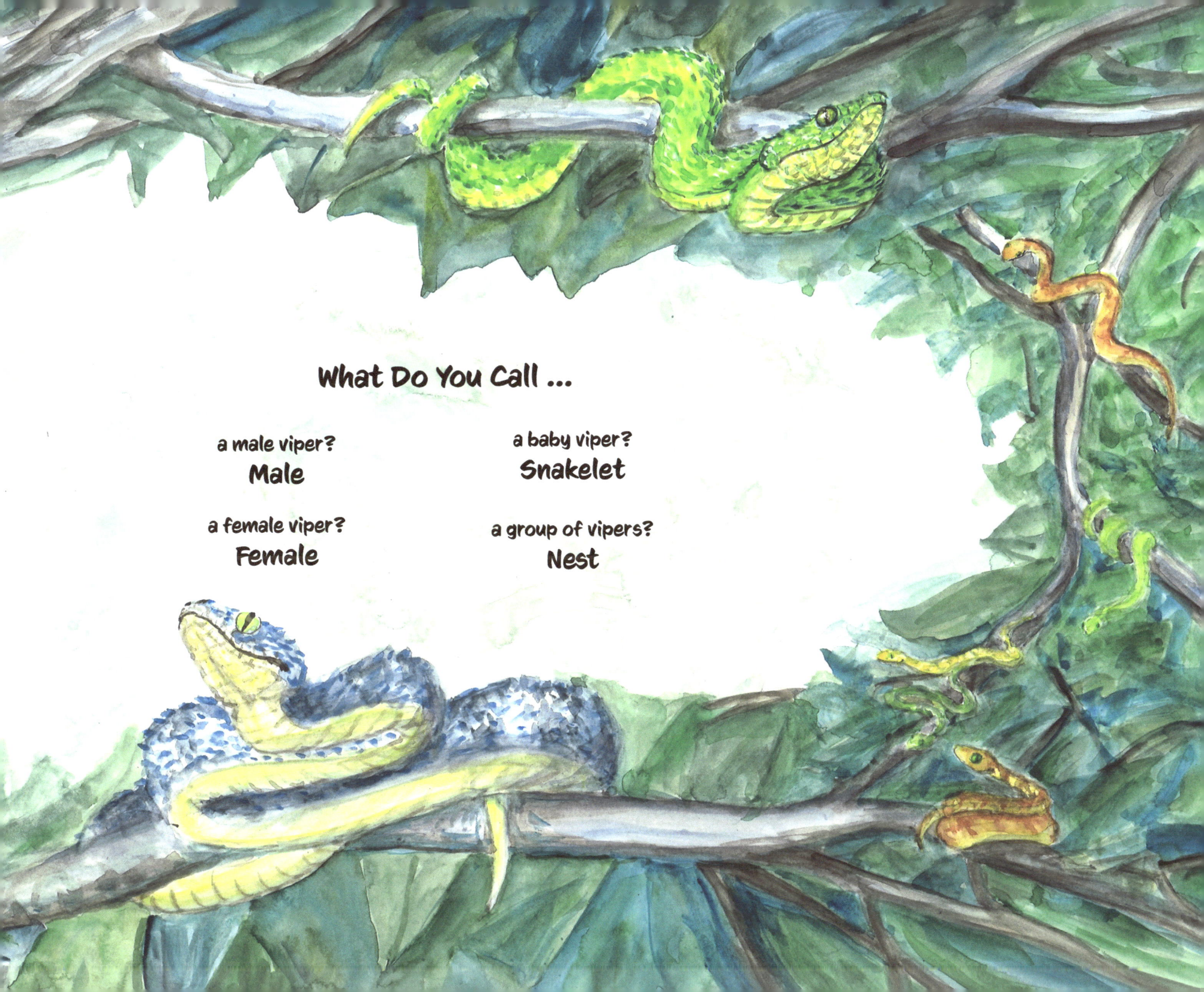

What Do You Call ...

a male viper?
Male

a baby viper?
Snakelet

a female viper?
Female

a group of vipers?
Nest

Wild Boar

Originated from islands in Southeast Asia such as Indonesia and the Philippines, and subsequently spread onto mainland Eurasia and North Africa.

Where they live: Europe, Africa, Asia; introduced into the United States, and also throughout the world.

Types of environment: Grassland and scrub to forest.

Diet: Wild boars eat shrubs, weeds, bird eggs, snakes, grasshoppers, mice, roots, tubers, even manure. Wild boars eat almost anything that will fit in their mouths.

What Do You Call ...

a male wild boar?
Boar

a baby wild boar?
Boarlet

a female wild boar?
Sow

a group of wild boars?
Sounder

The Center for Science Teaching and Learning (www.cstl.org) is a non-profit organization with a mission of encouraging science learning and literacy. CSTL conducts programs locally on Long Island, NY and globally. Scientists and science educators work together to bring engaging programs to families and students.

Special thanks go to
Rony Kessler
and Ryan Ridder